Across

1. Not dirty
2. Fashionable and interesting
3. Showing much knowledge
4. A foolish idea
5. Said or thought by some people to be the stated bad or illegal thing, although you have no proof
6. Containing, tasting of, or similar to nuts
7. Large in size or amount
8. Dissolves materials

Down

9. Not far away in distance
10. Unkind, cruel, without sympathy
11. Abnormal, deviant, different
12. Loved very much
13. Ordinary or usual
14. Disappointed discovering the truth
15. Respecting God
16. Boring
17. Complicated and difficult to solve
18. Unwilling to give information

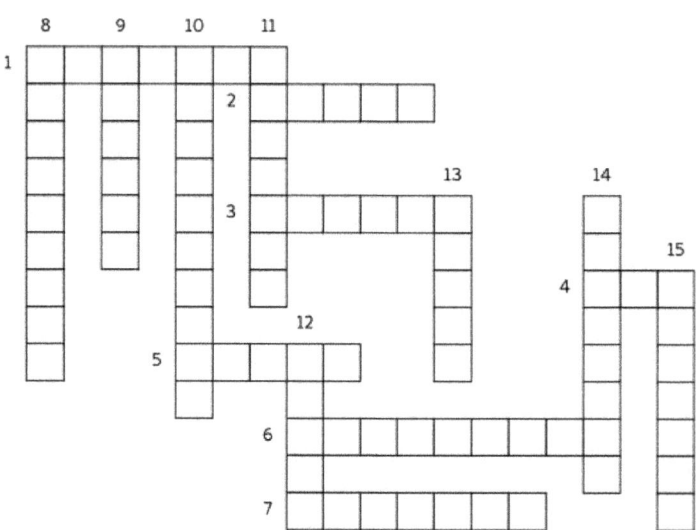

Across

1. Extremely surprising, very good, extremely surprised
2. Shaped like a ball or circle
3. Fact that everyone knows
4. Unhappy or sorry
5. At the same height
6. Limited to only one person
7. Revealing

Down

8. Able to be obtained, used, or reached
9. Stupid,unreasonable, silly in a humorous way, things that happen that are unreasonable
10. Impossible to defeat
11. Complain in an angry way
12. Develop
13. Containing, tasting of, or similar to nuts
14. Careful not to attract too much attention
15. Refusing to obey

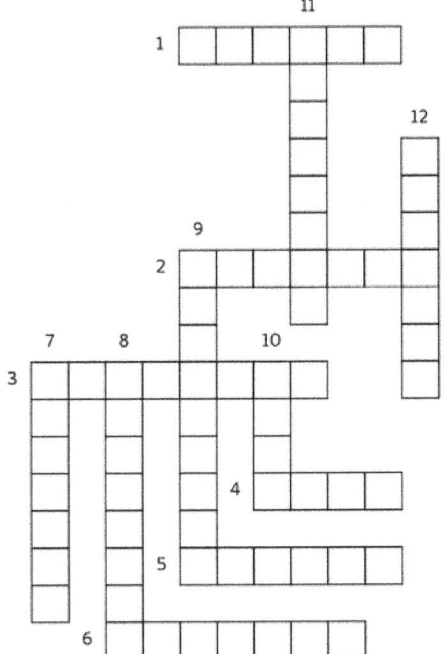

Across

1. Happening or done quickly and without warning
2. Officer
3. Inside the body
4. Boring
5. Rightened or worried
6. Showing much knowledge

Down

7. A foolish idea
8. Happy or grateful because of something
9. Habit of talking a lot
10. Dissolves materials
11. Careful not to attract too much attention
12. Revealing

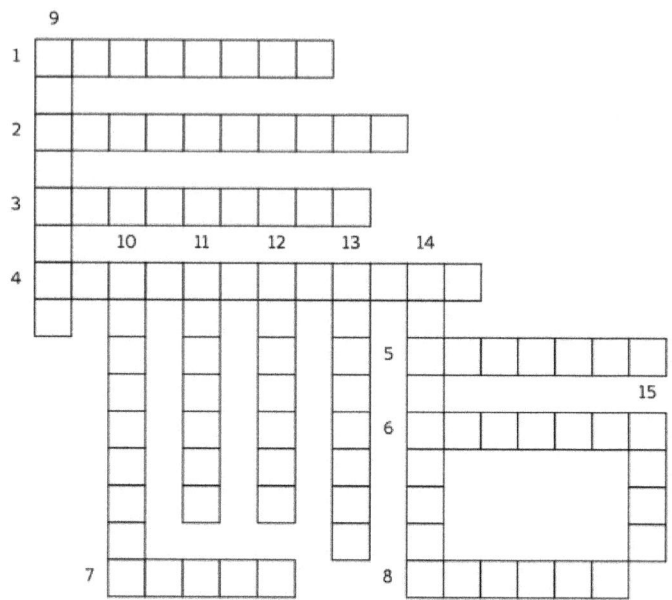

Across

1. Losing against someone
2. Making you feel pleased by providing what you need or want
3. Morally correct
4. Feeling of energetic interest
5. Unusual and unexpected
6. Harmed or spoiled
7. Develop
8. Rightened or worried

Down

9. Careful not to attract too much attention
10. Attractive or pleasant
11. Not armed
12. A foolish idea
13. Ability to do an activity or job well
14. Gradually and secretly causing harm
15. Boring

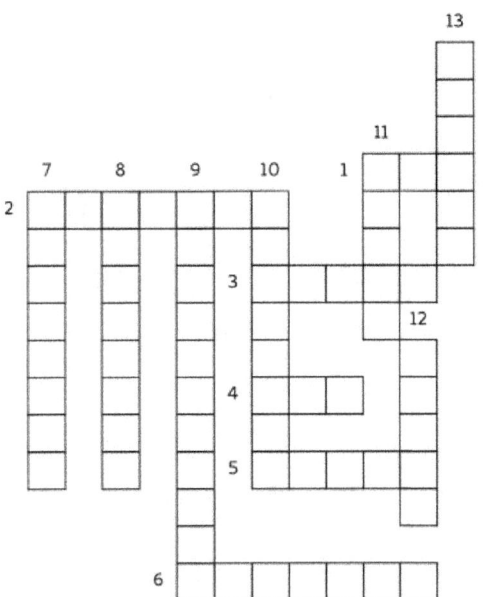

Across

1. Unhappy or sorry
2. Extremely surprising, very good, extremely surprised
3. At the same height
4. Large in size or amount
5. Develop
6. Attractive in appearance

Down

7. Abnormal, deviant, different
8. Someone who is trying to become successful
9. Eager to know a lot
10. Easily deceived
11. Not bitter or salty
12. Containing, tasting of, or similar to nuts
13. Happening or done quickly and without warning

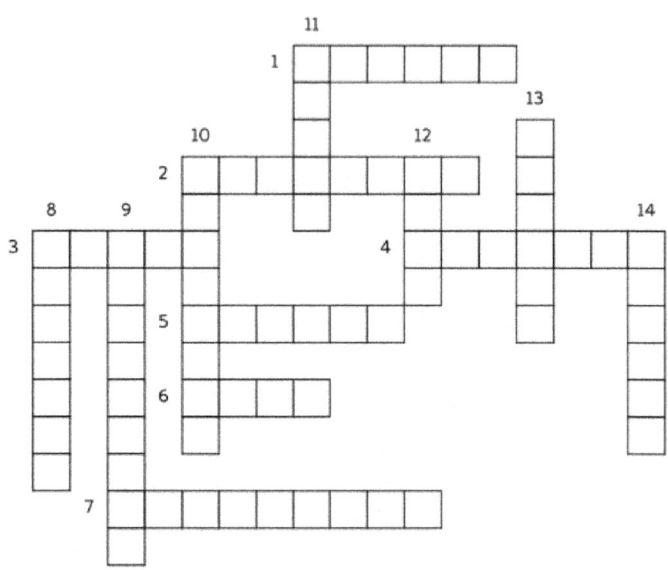

Across

1. Not difficult
2. Inside the body
3. Not dirty
4. A foolish idea
5. Fact that everyone knows
6. Not far away in distance
7. Gradually and secretly causing harm

Down

8. Unkind, cruel, without sympathy
9. Having a lot of energy
10. Not guilty of aparticular crime
11. Not bitter or salty
12. Dissolves materials
13. Fashionable and interesting
14. Rounded in a pleasant and attractive way

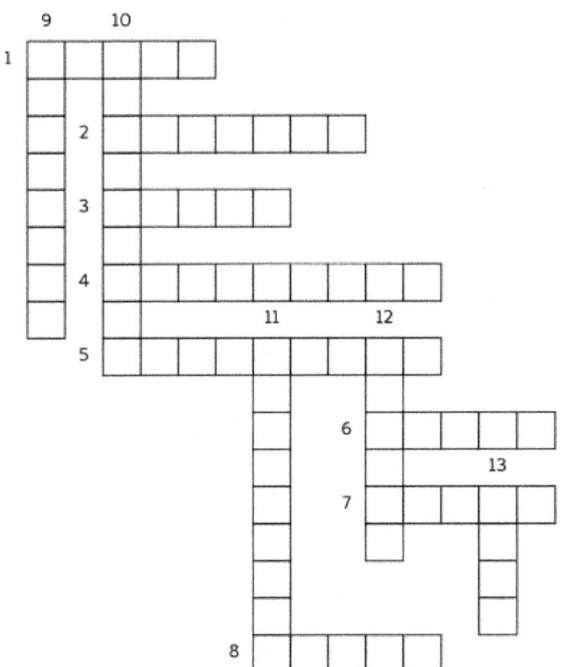

Across

1. Feel slightly drunk
2. Stopping and starting repeatedly
3. Shaped like a ball or circle
4. Limited to only one person
5. Attractive or pleasant
6. Not smooth
7. Telling not the true
8. Not bitter or salty

Down

9. Very respected
10. Detestable, repugnant, repulsive, morally very bad
11. Extremely funny
12. a phone who uses that
13. Not far away in distance

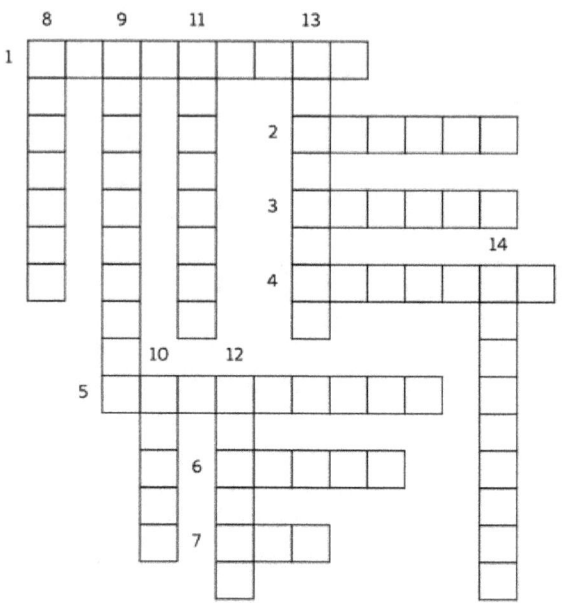

Across

1. Attractive or pleasant
2. Very happy
3. Immediately after the first and before any others
4. A foolish idea
5. Not wanting others to know
6. Not smooth
7. Unhappy or sorry

Down

8. Revealing
9. Unacceptable, offensive, violent, or unusual
10. Develop
11. Physically attractive
12. Strong and unlikely to break or fail
13. Beautiful, powerful, or causing great admiration and respect
14. Gradually and secretly causing harm

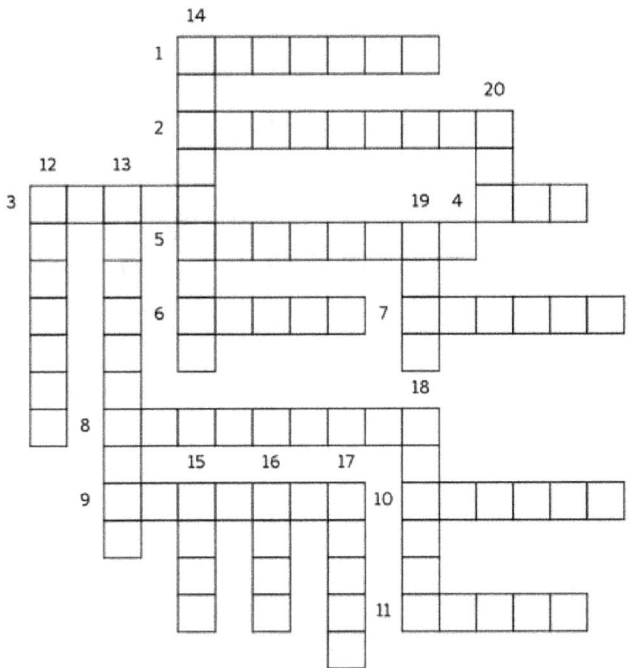

Across

1. Extremely surprising, very good, extremely surprised
2. Morally correct
3. Complete or not divided
4. No water or other liquid in
5. Someone who is trying to become successful
6. At the same height
7. Poor, unsuccessful, the state of being extremely unhappy
8. Having a lot of energy
9. Not armed
10. Behave like adults
11. Containing, tasting of, or similar to nuts

Down

12. Not having something
13. Unacceptable, offensive, violent, or unusual
14. Accepted, accept something
15. Dissolves materials
16. Man
17. Drinking too much alcohol
18. Fact that everyone knows
19. Not far away in distance
20. Unhappy or sorry

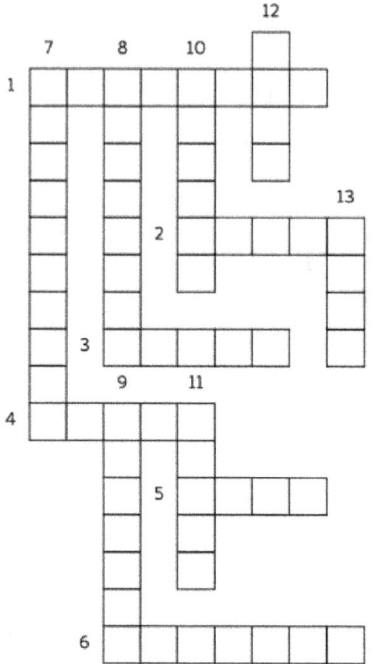

Across

1. Careful not to attract too much attention
2. Hard or firm
3. At the same height
4. Telling not the true
5. Loved very much
6. Attractive in appearance

Down

7. Very pleasant
8. Ability to do an activity or job well
9. Extremely large
10. Strong and unlikely to break or fail
11. Respecting God
12. Not physically strong
13. Boring

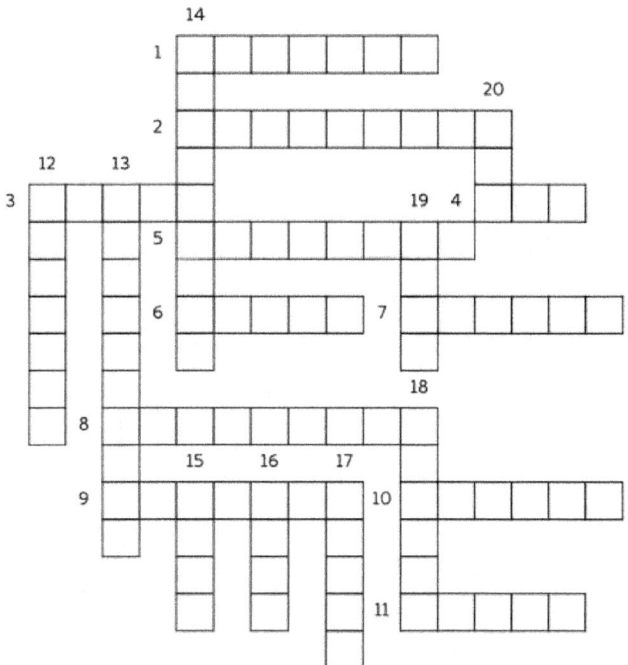

Across

1. Extremely surprising, very good, extremely surprised
2. Morally correct
3. Complete or not divided
4. No water or other liquid in
5. Someone who is trying to become successful
6. At the same height
7. Poor, unsuccessful, the state of being extremely unhappy
8. Having a lot of energy
9. Not armed
10. Behave like adults
11. Containing, tasting of, or similar to nuts

Down

12. Not having something
13. Unacceptable, offensive, violent, or unusual
14. Accepted, accept something
15. Dissolves materials
16. Man
17. Drinking too much alcohol
18. Fact that everyone knows
19. Not far away in distance
20. Unhappy or sorry

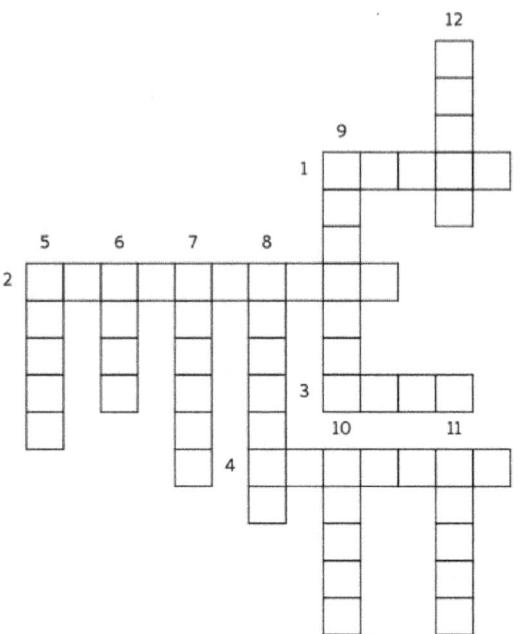

Across

1. Causing pain intentionally
2. Very well
3. Not in danger or likely to be harmed
4. Revealing

Down

5. Unkind, cruel
6. Not far away in distance
7. Rightened or worried
8. Gigantic prehistoric animal
9. Unkind, cruel, without sympathy
10. Telling not the true
11. Containing, tasting of, or similar to nuts
12. Not bitter or salty

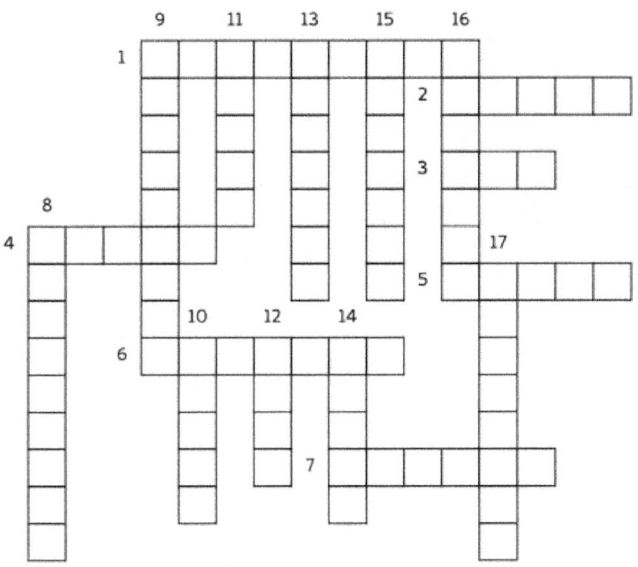

Across

1. Limited to only one person
2. Telling not the true
3. Unhappy or sorry
4. Not bitter or salty
5. Unwilling to give information
6. Full of people
7. Rounded in a pleasant and attractive way

Down

8. Not wanting others to know
9. Having a lot of energy
10. Shaped like a ball or circle
11. Causing pain intentionally
12. Not physically strong
13. Not armed
14. Develop
15. Extremely large
16. Able to stretch
17. Attractive, appealing, lovely, charming, and easily loved

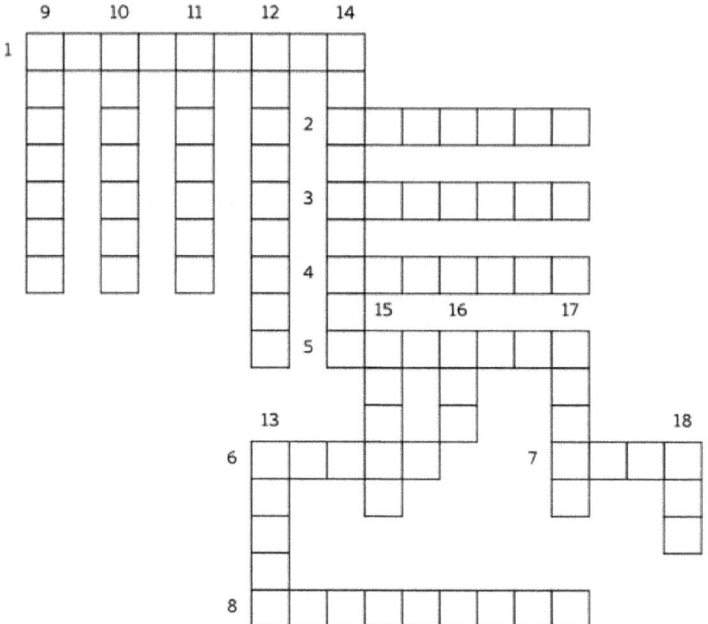

Across

1. Eager to fight or argue
2. Difficult to understand
3. Not armed
4. A foolish idea
5. Able to stretch
6. Not bitter or salty
7. Dissolves materials
8. Feeling extreme dislike

Down

9. Unkind, cruel, without sympathy
10. Gigantic prehistoric animal
11. Extremely surprising, very good, extremely surprised
12. Gradually and secretly causing harm
13. Hard or firm
14. Limited to only one person
15. At the same height
16. Unhappy or sorry
17. Easy to understand
18. No water or other liquid in

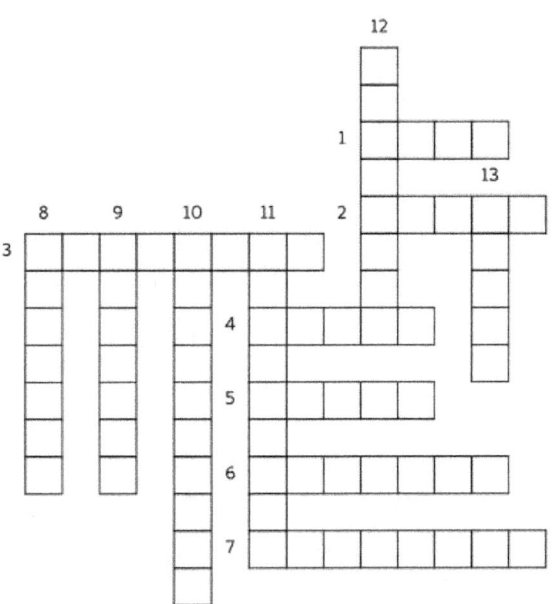

Across

1. Nothing more than
2. Telling not the true
3. Inside the body
4. Unkind, cruel
5. Shaped like a ball or circle
6. Attractive in appearance
7. Happy or grateful because of something

Down

8. Extremely large
9. Revealing
10. Able to send back light a surface
11. Detestable, repugnant, repulsive, morally very bad
12. Without a home
13. Containing, tasting of, or similar to nuts

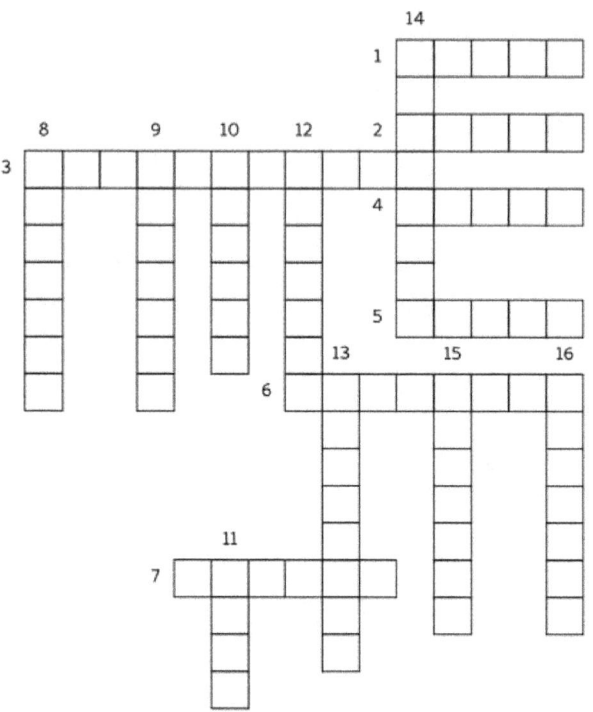

Across
1. Easy to understand
2. Develop
3. Eager to know a lot
4. Shaped like a ball or circle
5. Telling not the true
6. Expressing thanks
7. Complicated and difficult to solve

Down
8. Extremely large
9. Not armed
10. Happening or done quickly and without warning
11. Not far away in distance
12. Revealing
13. Relating to love or a close loving relationship
14. Happy and positive
15. Attractive in appearance
16. Showing much knowledge

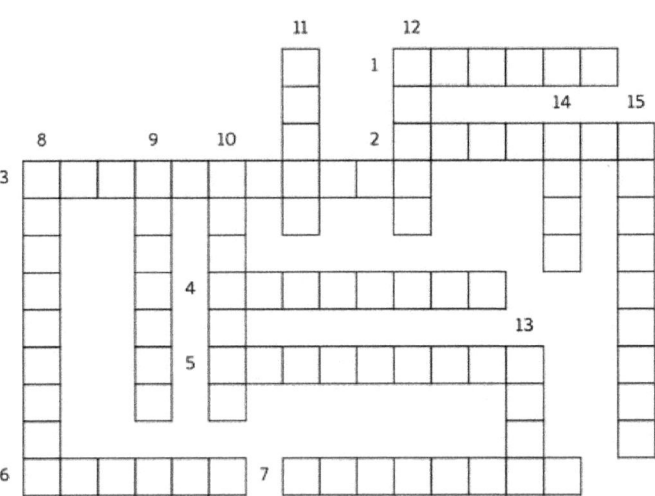

Across

1. Immediately after the first and before any others
2. Attractive in appearance
3. Eager to know a lot
4. Abnormal, deviant, different
5. Habit of talking a lot
6. Happening or done quickly and without warning
7. Careful not to attract too much attention

Down

8. Gradually and secretly causing harm
9. Not armed
10. Unusual and unexpected
11. Containing, tasting of, or similar to nuts
12. Not bitter or salty
13. Not in danger or likely to be harmed
14. Dissolves materials
15. Attractive or pleasant

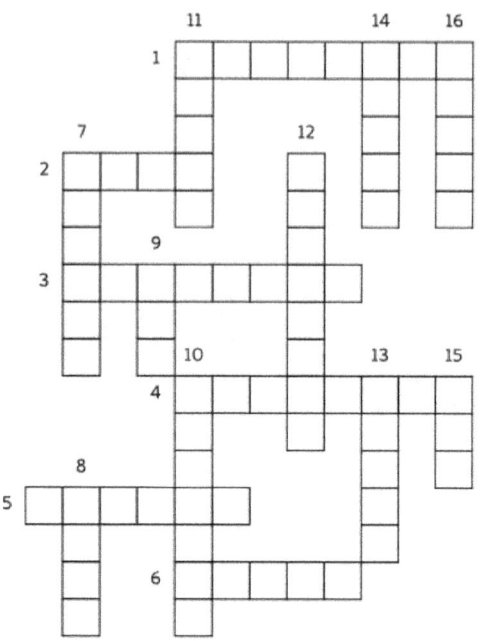

Across

1. Ability to do an activity or job well
2. Not in danger or likely to be harmed
3. Careful not to attract too much attention
4. Very respected
5. Complicated and difficult to solve
6. Containing, tasting of, or similar to nuts

Down

7. Happening or done quickly and without warning
8. Not far away in distance
9. Unhappy or sorry
10. Stopping and starting repeatedly
11. Not bitter or salty
12. Young person
13. Complete or not divided
14. Coming before all others
15. No water or other liquid in
16. At the same height

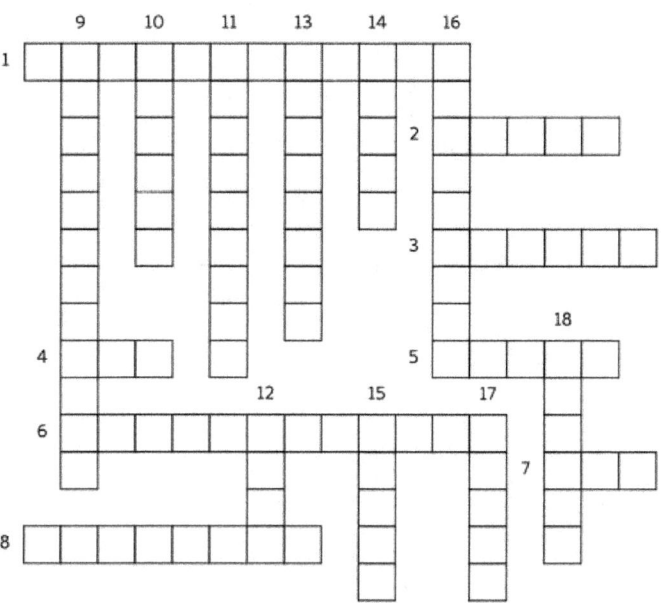

Across

1. Not certain, or wrong in some way
2. Causing pain intentionally
3. Happening or done quickly and without warning
4. Unhappy or sorry
5. Develop
6. Feeling of energetic interest
7. Large in size or amount
8. Careful not to attract too much attention

Down

9. Not excited
10. Rightened or worried
11. Gradually and secretly causing harm
12. Not in danger or likely to be harmed
13. Not clear and having no form
14. The color of chocolate
15. Not bitter or salty
16. Limited to only one person
17. Not dirty
18. Rounded in a pleasant and attractive way

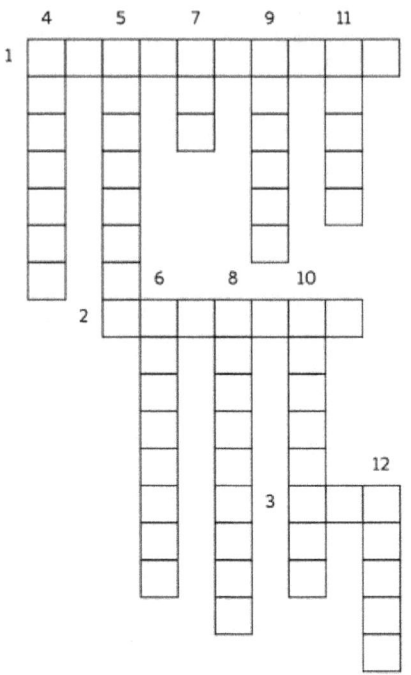

Across

1. Very well
2. Unusual and unexpected
3. Large in size or amount

Down

4. Extremely ugly or bad
5. Not clear and having no form
6. Happy or grateful because of something
7. Unhappy or sorry
8. Detestable, repugnant, repulsive, morally very bad
9. Behave like adults
10. Easily deceived
11. At the same height
12. Respecting God

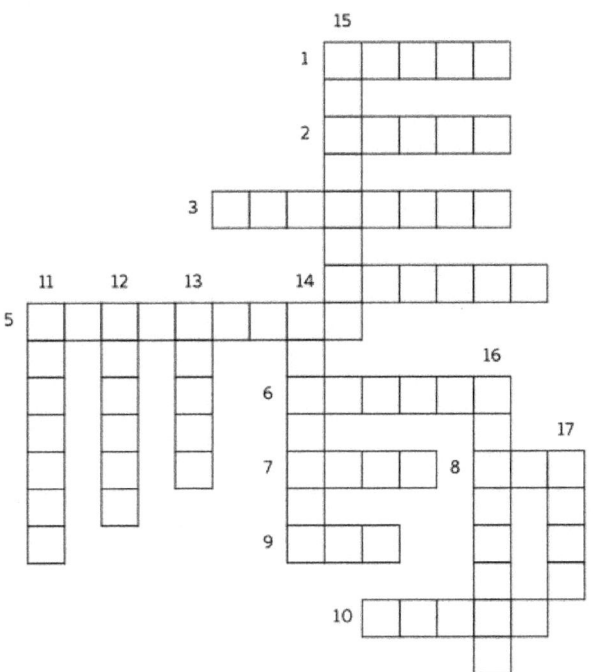

Across

1. Unkind, cruel
2. Dark and dirty or difficult to see through
3. Easily deceived
4. Not difficult
5. Hing, or activity could harm you
6. On or onto a ship, aircraft, bus, or train
7. Man
8. Unhappy or sorry
9. No water or other liquid in
10. Not bitter or salty

Down

11. Refusing to obey
12. Ordinary or usual
13. Develop
14. Not armed
15. Without a home
16. Careful not to attract too much attention
17. Loved very much

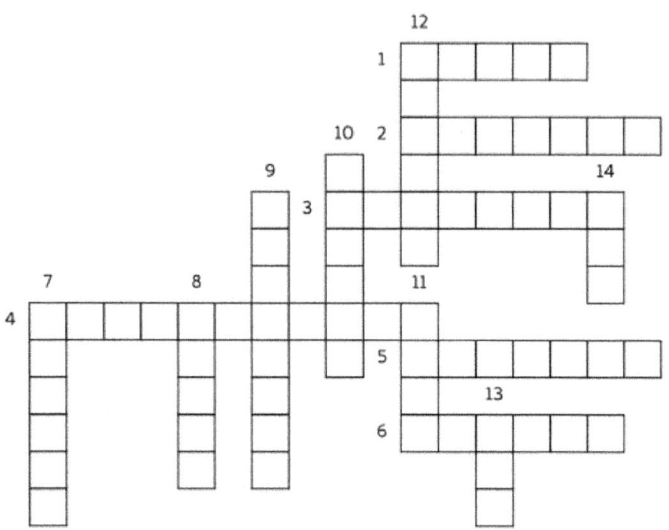

Across

1. Unwilling to give information
2. Not armed
3. Not clear and having no form
4. Trying to seem very important
5. Attractive in appearance
6. Strong and unlikely to break or fail

Down

7. Ordinary
8. Coming before all others
9. Easily deceived
10. Complicated and difficult to solve
11. Not far away in distance
12. Rounded in a pleasant and attractive way
13. Large in size or amount
14. Unhappy or sorry

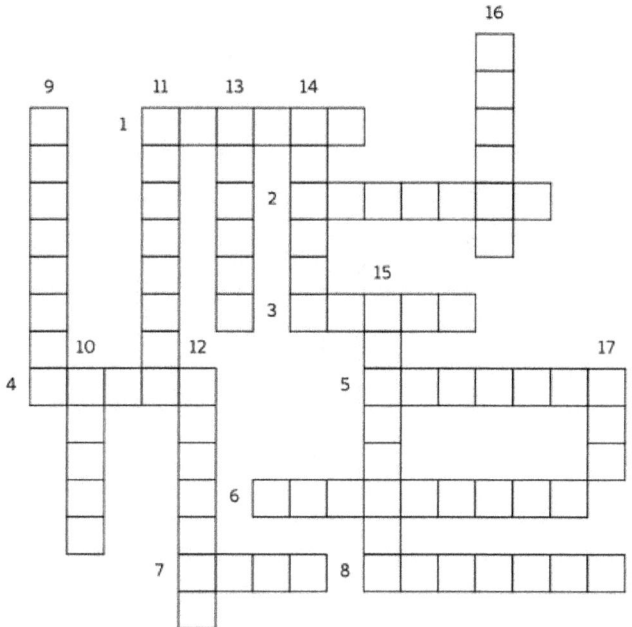

Across

1. Poor, unsuccessful, the state of being extremely unhappy
2. Gigantic prehistoric animal
3. Containing, tasting of, or similar to nuts
4. Not bitter or salty
5. Said or thought by some people to be the stated bad or illegal thing, although you have no proof
6. Not the same
7. Not far away in distance
8. Showing much knowledge

Down

9. Without a home
10. Not correct
11. Glue
12. Revealing
13. Very happy
14. Fact that everyone knows
15. Happy or grateful because of something
16. Complicated and difficult to solve
17. No water or other liquid in

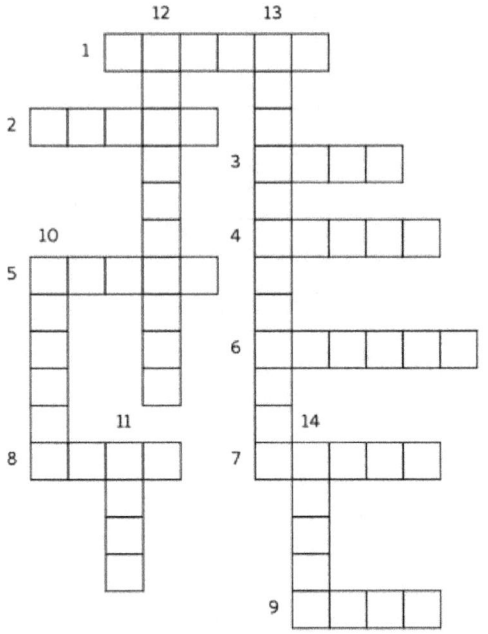

Across

1. Very happy
2. Containing, tasting of, or similar to nuts
3. Not far away in distance
4. Develop
5. Not bitter or salty
6. Not difficult
7. Drinking too much alcohol
8. Loved very much
9. Boring

Down

10. Immediately after the first and before any others
11. Dissolves materials
12. Unacceptable, offensive, violent, or unusual
13. Not excited
14. Shaped like a ball or circle

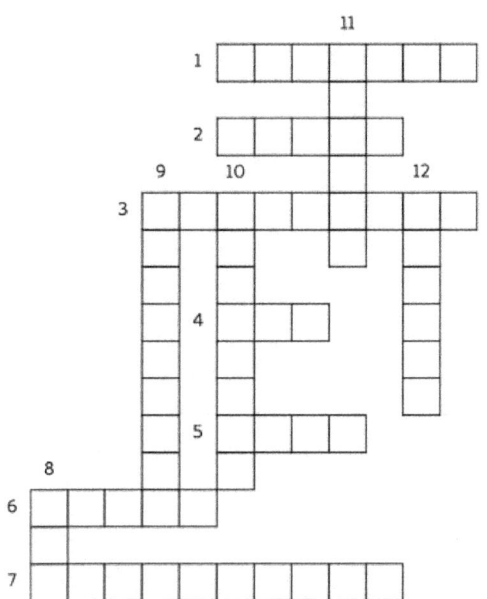

Across

1. Gigantic prehistoric animal
2. Containing, tasting of, or similar to nuts
3. Detestable, repugnant, repulsive, morally very bad
4. No water or other liquid in
5. Nothing more than
6. Not bitter or salty
7. Very pleasant

Down

8. Unhappy or sorry
9. Able to be obtained, used, or reached
10. Physically attractive
11. Behave like adults
12. Ordinary or usual

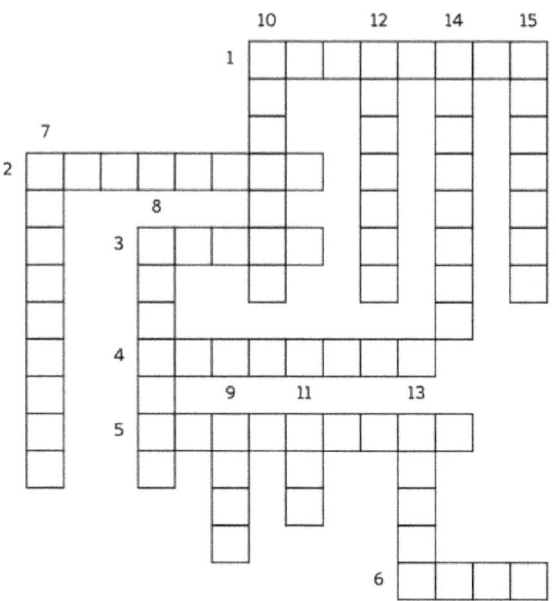

Across

1. Having a pleasant smell
2. Careful not to attract too much attention
3. Not bitter or salty
4. Excited, interested, enthusiastic
5. Grand very large
6. Loved very much

Down

7. Hing, or activity could harm you
8. Unusual and unexpected
9. Dissolves materials
10. Said or thought by some people to be the stated bad or illegal thing, although you have no proof
11. No water or other liquid in
12. Gigantic prehistoric animal
13. Hard or firm
14. Happy or grateful because of something
15. Unkind, cruel, without sympathy

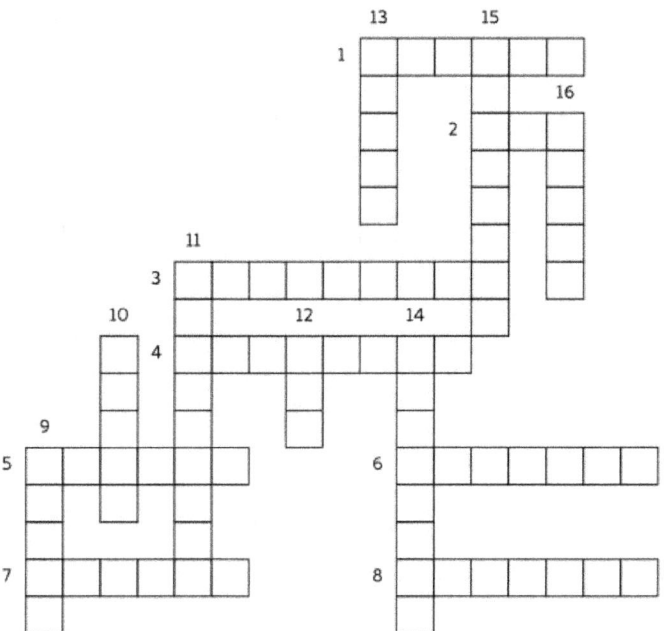

Across

1. Happening or done quickly and without warning
2. Unhappy or sorry
3. Able to be obtained, used, or reached
4. Physically attractive
5. Behave like adults
6. Able to stretch
7. Complicated and difficult to solve
8. Extremely large

Down

9. Dark and dirty or difficult to see through
10. Containing, tasting of, or similar to nuts
11. Detestable, repugnant, repulsive, morally very bad
12. No water or other liquid in
13. Not bitter or salty
14. Beautiful, powerful, or causing great admiration and respect
15. Careful not to attract too much attention
16. Drinking too much alcohol

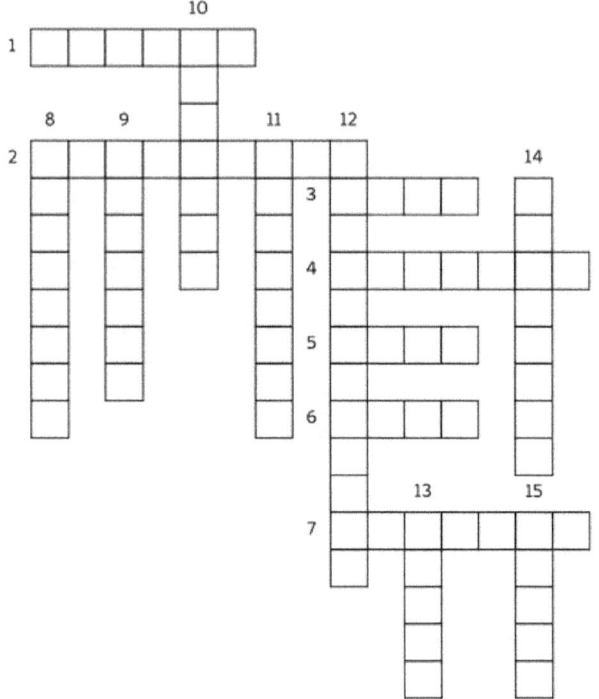

Across

1. Complicated and difficult to solve
2. Able to be obtained, used, or reached
3. Not far away in distance
4. Stopping and starting repeatedly
5. Not in danger or likely to be harmed
6. Dissolves materials
7. Extremely large

Down

8. Having a pleasant smell
9. Extremely surprising, very good, extremely surprised
10. Revealing
11. Become pink in the face
12. Feeling of energetic interest
13. Dark and dirty or difficult to see through
14. Not guilty of aparticular crime
15. Not bitter or salty

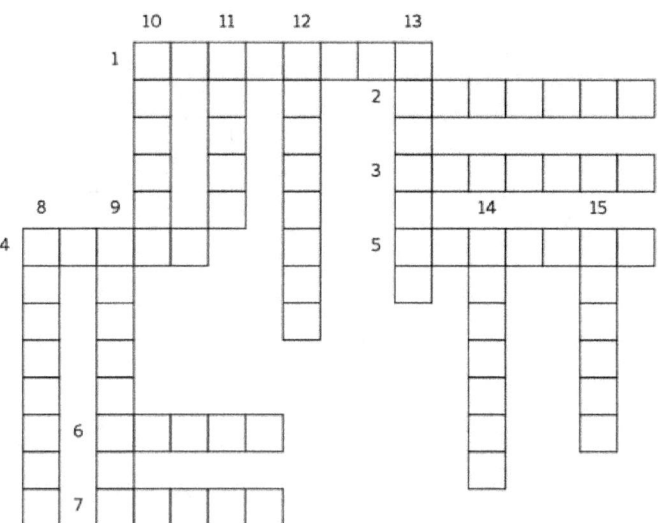

Across

1. Glue
2. Showing much knowledge
3. Unusual and unexpected
4. Containing, tasting of, or similar to nuts
5. Extremely large
6. Coming before all others
7. At the same height

Down

8. Not clear and having no form
9. Happy or grateful because of something
10. Poor, unsuccessful, the state of being extremely unhappy
11. Feel slightly drunk
12. Ability to do an activity or job well
13. Able to stretch
14. Gigantic prehistoric animal
15. Rightened or worried

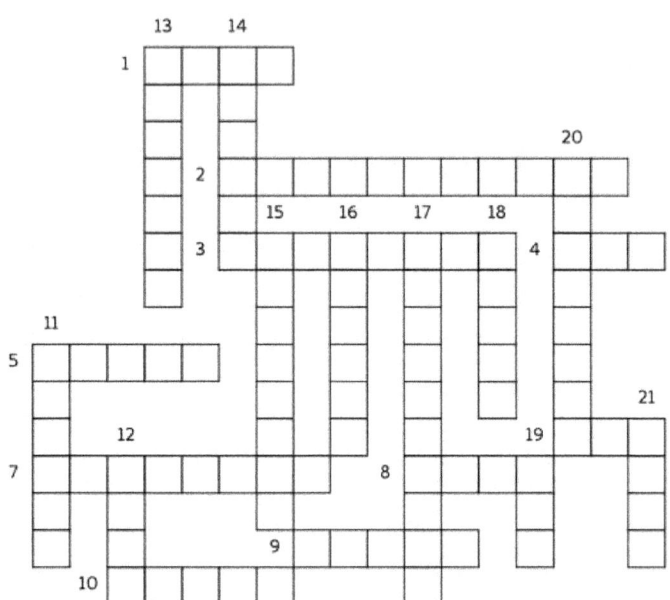

Across

1. Boring
2. Make something more likely to happen
3. Happy or grateful because of something
4. Large in size or amount
5. Hard or firm
6. Unhappy or sorry
7. Careful not to attract too much attention
8. Dissolves materials
9. Not bitter or salty
10. Develop

Down

11. Happening or done quickly and without warning
12. Not in danger or likely to be harmed
13. Harmed or spoiled
14. Poor, unsuccessful, the state of being extremely unhappy
15. Very respected
16. Ordinary or usual
17. Extremely interested
18. Telling not the true
19. No water or other liquid in
20. Not clear and having no form
21. Loved very much

www.ingramcontent.com/pod-product-compliance
Lightning Source LLC
Chambersburg PA
CBHW072227290526
45794CB00007B/2922